TIDEWATER VIRGINIA
IN COLOR

TIDEWATER

VIRGINIA

in Color

TEXT BY PARKE ROUSE, JR.

HASTINGS HOUSE · PUBLISHERS

New York

For my father

PUBLISHED 1968 BY HASTINGS HOUSE, PUBLISHERS, INC.

Reprinted February, 1976
Reprinted April, 1980
Reprinted March, 1988

Library of Congress Catalog Card Number 68-16003

ISBN Number: 8038-7066-3

Printed and bound in Hong Kong by Mandarin Offset

Distributed to the trade by:

Kampmann & Co., Inc., New York, NY

CONTENTS

ACKNOWLEDGMENTS

VIRGINIA is notable for the number of its historic buildings preserved by private owners or historical societies. All those depicted in this book are open to the public except the Saint George Tucker House, Brandon and Westover. In the case of the latter two, the gardens and outbuildings are open, though not the residences themselves.

The author wishes to express thanks to the photographers who made their work available. These include Mr. Frank Dementi of Colonial Studios, Richmond; Mr. Anthony L. Dementi of Dementi Studios, Richmond; Mr. Philip Flournoy of the Virginia State Chamber of Commerce, Richmond; Mr. Walter H. Miller of Williamsburg; and Mr. Samuel Chamberlain of Marblehead, Massachusetts. Appreciation for the use of pictures is also expressed to Colonial Williamsburg and to the Virginian Department of Conservation and Development.

P.R., JR.

O F ALL THE BAYS which offer haven to ships along the Atlantic coast, the Chesapeake is the largest. For this reason the English chose to begin their seventeenth-century penetration of the New World there. Its vast reaches offered ready-made sea roads to the merchant ships of London and Bristol, and the westerly bent of its rivers encouraged the hope that one of them spanned the continent to the Pacific and the riches of the Orient beyond.

Alas, the fabled Northwest Passage was never found. Instead, however, the settlers discovered a pine-forested land cut into countless green peninsulas. An endless maze of rivers and creeks irrigated this "new English nation", as Sir Walter Raleigh called it, and linked it with Mother England 3750 miles away. Here, then, began the English settlement of North America which was to lead to the British Commonwealth of Nations and the United States of America.

Tidewater Virginia had a unique geography, and in the first 200 years of English settlement it developed a unique civilization. The sparkling blue Chesapeake was its core, flowing into the Atlantic between Cape Henry and Cape Charles. Into this maritime corridor there emptied dozens of tidal creeks and rivers, teeming with fish, crabs and oysters. The largest of these estuaries formed an arc, like the fingers projecting from a hand, which drained the massive interior of Virginia.

It was along these rivers—the James, York, Piankatank,

Rappahannock and Potomac—that the early settlements huddled. Discouraged in their hope of discovering a passage to the Pacific or of finding gold, the Englishmen turned to the cultivation of tobacco, which Rolfe had first tried at Jamestown in 1612. Once the tobacco trade was established, a growing number of Englishmen took advantage of the Virginia Company's offer of fifty acres per head and settled in Virginia. Wherever they could, they chose land fronting on deep water so that ships could discharge English goods and load Virginia tobacco from the owner's dock.

For a hundred years the fall-line formed the western boundary of this civilization. Ships could not go up the rivers beyond these falls, and the shipping of tobacco above them was therefore difficult and expensive. Thus the plantation society developed an economic unity which led to social homogeneity. This coastal belt stretched approximately a hundred miles inland, from the twin sentinels of Cape Henry and Cape Charles on the coast to the fall-line on the west, where later grew the towns of Petersburg, Richmond, Fredericksburg and Alexandria.

Even after settlement in the eighteenth century pushed inland beyond the fall-line, Tidewater continued to dominate the affairs of the colony. All of Virginia's seventeenth-century leaders and most of her Revolutionary heroes were Tidewater men. The Tidewater bloc became so powerful that it resisted almost until the Civil War the inevitable gravitation of Virginia's power center toward the west. In fact, the resistance of Tidewater statesmen to the demands of the trans-Alleghany counties of Virginia contributed to the secession of West Virginia from the Old Dominion in 1863.

In all periods of history, the established civilization of the coastal lowland has looked down upon the newer citizens of the interior. So it was in ancient Greece. So it was in the Mediterranean basin in the Middle Ages. And so it was in early America.

Virginia was no exception. Indeed the sea-girt isolation of Tidewater's peninsulas bred a pride and provincialism in early Virginians which has never washed out. They called themselves Cavaliers and their state The Old Dominion to identify themselves with the Royalists in England's Civil War. They frankly copied the homes and habits of England's squires. They likened their slave-supported plantations to England's manors. And like the ancient Greeks, they saw no conflict between aristocracy and democracy. They believed in both.

It was a gentle land, inhabited by gentle people, and it has been slow to change. Its rivers discouraged road-building and railways, and this lack of communication in turn delayed the coming of factories. Well into the twentieth century, river boats provided a major part of its transport, hauling the money crops of tobacco and cotton, plus fish, lumber and truck crops. Only after World War I did the rural face of Tidewater clearly begin to give way to the Industrial Revolution.

Even today much of Tidewater Virginia sticks serenely to rural life, even though a great industrial megalopolis, from Boston southward to Norfolk, is pressing down upon it.

Tidewater Virginia has been slow to industrialize because its water barriers have deterred new ideas, new enterprises and new residents. The oldest of its settlements, of course, took place on *the* Peninsula, between the James and the York. Next to be inhabited was the land south of the James, long known as Southside Virginia. The third area to be settled was the promontory between the York and Rappahannock rivers, paralleling the Peninsula.

After that came settlements in the lordly Northern Neck, bounded on one side by the Rappahannock and on the other by the Potomac and the shore of Maryland. A fifth area, remote from the rest of Tidewater, is the Eastern Shore, which falls southward from Maryland like a raccoon's tail. During the 1960's these five regions finally have been linked by bridges and tunnels. The visitor now sees them as one continuous highway system. Actually, they are five separate principalities, each a law unto itself.

Virginia's coast at first glance looks drab compared to the wild and rocky shore of New England. Most of it is low, flat and marshy. However, the very tameness of its waterways makes them inviting. Along the Atlantic, the beaches are wide and golden, with hillocks of sea oats shimmering in the sun. Sand dunes, whipped up by ocean winds, crowd the shoreline and offer haven to bayberry, saltbush and live-oak trees, which bend landward like taut Japanese pines.

As one progresses up Chesapeake Bay and Hampton Roads, the beaches narrow and give way to marsh. In many places pine forests rise sheer from the shoreline. A few ancient cypress trees grow up from the water around the Dismal Swamp. Once this picturesque and durable giant lined many Virginia rivers, but woodsmen have cut most of it for houses and ships.

The marshes that clog Virginia's creeks have developed since the white man came. His clearing of land along the shores caused topsoil to erode into the rivers. In turgid shoal water, cattails now grow in wild profusion, offering haven for millions of redwing blackbirds, muskrats, raccoons, otters and sand crabs. During the migrations of songbirds along the Atlantic flyways through Virginia, these swamps come alive with feathered singers. Fall brings flocks of duck and geese southward from Canada, stopping to rest and feed in marshes surrounding Back Bay, the Mattaponi, the Pamunkey and the Chickahominy.

The greening of these lowlands in spring and their darkening to brown and gray in fall is one of the delights of the Tidewater landscape.

The tidal waters continue to provide livelihood for many men, as they have done since the Jamestown colony sent settlers to the Eastern Shore in 1614 to catch and salt down fish for its use. Once sturgeon abounded. Today's catches are chiefly of herring and shad, which unerringly return from the ocean each spring and swim upstream to the very creeks where they were spawned. The herringlike menhaden is widely netted for its oil, and many other species are caught by net and handline for table use.

Rivers are pocked with pound nets, which fishermen arrange in rows athwart the tide to drive schooling fish into net corrals and there to trap them. The earliest Virginians learned this from the Indians. They also learned from the savages to make purse-shaped fish traps, open at one end and baited to attract sea-bottom scavengers. From this trap evolved the lobster pot and the wire-mesh crab pot, whose blue-bottle markers bedevil boatmen who travel the Chesapeake tributaries.

Chesapeake Bay oysters long have been recognized as one of God's gifts to man. Hundreds of watermen still make a living dredging these crustaceans in winter, after netting fish in spring and summer. The transplanting of seed oysters from the fabulously productive James River beds gives seasonal employment when all else fails.

There are few Tidewater Virginians who have not lain abed in the darkness of a fall morning and heard the lonely *putt-putt-putt* of the

12

oysterman's boat, making its way from a snug harbour through choppy waters to the oyster rocks. These grizzled optimists are the ruggedest individuals surviving in twentieth-century America. Working from before sunup to late afternoon, they brave the Chesapeake in all seasons in their tiny boats. With long oyster tongs, they grapple for shellfish submerged beneath ten feet of water.

Many of these Neptunes have inherited boat, nets, tongs and crab pots from their fathers. Though their life is precarious, it offers freedom and adventure. (Besides, tax officials have no way of knowing how much cash they receive annually from seafood-buying companies!) In their white clapboard villages centering around a church—usually Methodist—they live an insulated life and speak in Elizabethan accents. The typical watermen of Gloucester County's Guinea Marsh treat outsiders with cool suspicion. Who knows what visitor may be a revenue man, a fisheries inspector or a professor who wants to record their archaic speech?

Every port has its peculiar boats. The Chesapeake is no exception. The all-purpose carrier of today's cargoes is the skipjack, a sailboat whose dead-rise hull can haul a heavy catch even in rough seas. Nearly extinct is the bugeye, a shapely two-masted vessel, whose hull was cut from seven or nine pine logs fitted together longitudinally. Even rarer is the Chesapeake Bay canoe, which was hollowed from three or five logs in imitation of the Indians' log canoes.

The commercial use of Tidewater's rivers has ebbed steadily in the automatic age. Plantation docks that lined the rivers have disappeared. Countless river towns that had come into being as ports gradually lost their shipping as steamships grew too large for their channels. In some cases rivers have been clogged by silt and swamps; in the nineteenth century it became impossible for sailing ships to reach Williamsburg by Queens or College Creek. Gradually such inland ports as Suffolk, Smithfield, Port Royal and Falmouth have given way to the deep-water harbors of Norfolk, Newport News, Richmond and Portsmouth.

Tidewater's rivers have evolved from a business asset into a recreational resource.

The eighty-mile peninsula which stretches from Old Point Comfort to Richmond was the first choice of Virginia's settlers. Here Virginia's three capitals have been located: Jamestown in the seventeenth century, Williamsburg until the Revolution and Richmond ever since. In this brief compass occurred an amazing number of crucial events in the history of the United States. Plantation houses still flank the turgid James. Pine forests alternate with croplands and pastures. Deer, quail, rabbits and wild duck find hospitable cover. An air of rustic peace is everywhere.

This is the peninsula that historian Lyon Gardiner Tyler called "the cradle of the republic". Today's visitor sees it much as the founding families left it: Carters, Burwells, Randolphs, Harrisons, Byrds, Tylers and others. At The Forest, in Charles City County, Thomas Jefferson married the widow Martha Wayles Skelton. At nearby Shirley, Anne Carter Lee brought her young son Robert Edward to visit his Carter grandparents. A few miles away, at peerless Westover, genteel William Byrd II read his daily stint of Greek, wrote learnedly to London pedants and confided his sins to a shorthand diary. (Like a kindred Virginian whose tombstone is at Jamestown, Byrd was "A Great Sinner, Confidently Awaiting a Joyful Resurrection".)

Those were the days when the James River plantations housed the most cultivated and admired life in the colonies. The era was born at Jamestown in 1612, when Rolfe grew his first tobacco. Then, for more than 200 years, the golden leaf spread over Virginia and the Carolinas to bring wealth to planters throughout the lowlands. But the heart of the agrarian South throughout colonial times remained the James River valley, whose docks linked Virginia with the Mother Country.

The earliest Peninsula plantations were simple, and few survive. Malvern Hill was built about 1662 in Henrico County, thirty miles west of Jamestown. In New Kent County, a few miles away, are Foster's Castle, built about 1685, and Criss Cross or Christ's Cross, a typical cross-shaped Jacobean house, built about 1690.

The famous era of Tidewater mansion-building began when Governor Sir William Berkeley developed palatial Green Spring near Jamestown between 1645 and 1676. Rich and well educated, Berkeley imported racehorses for his wilderness Versailles and kept an aristocratic ear cocked toward the Court and literary London. Typical of his crusty paternalism was his sneer, "I thank God there are no free schools nor printing, and I hope we shall not have these hundred years. . . ." This polished courtier was the English squire transplanted to Virginia. He influenced the tone of its country life for years to come.

After Berkeley's day, houses along the James grew grander. Carter Burwell began Carter's Grove near Williamsburg about 1746. Farther west, toward Richmond, an early Benjamin Harrison built Berkeley and a pioneer Carter built Shirley. On and on they went, as tobacco fortunes bourgeoned and families multiplied. Today the Peninsula from Williamsburg to Richmond, fifty miles to the west, boasts the finest array of Georgian country houses in America.

After the Revolution had wilted the tobacco economy, many Tidewater plantations fell on evil days. Some passed from their builders' hands. Others were leveled by fire or wantonness. Those that have survived the centuries are pearls of great price. When the last owner of Carter's Grove died in 1960, the Rockefeller brothers paid more than $1,000,000 to exhibit the house and thus to amplify the story of Williamsburg.

Carter's Grove illustrates the evolution of a Tidewater plantation. As tobacco culture moved southward from Jamestown, the first plantations switched to cotton and then to low-maintenance crops: small grains, soybeans, corn, cattle, sheep and pine trees. Even more rewarding than agriculture today are tourists who pay $1 or $1.50 each to visit these houses.

The men who built them had an eye for beauty as well as a knack for making money—and often for making rich marriages. On choice locations fronting the James and the York they built English-style houses of enduring beauty. Sometimes the houses were added to by successive generations. When fully developed, they usually included not only a manor house but a kitchen overseer's office, servants' quarters (never referred to as slave quarters), stable, icehouse, privies, smokehouse, barn and sometimes craft houses.

The earliest plantation houses were often built out of view of the river for security against Spanish attack, but most of the great eighteenth-century houses dared to face the river, as at Westover and Carter's Grove, the latter cited by expert Samuel Chamberlain as "the most beautiful house in America".

Battles of the Revolution and the Civil War dealt Peninsula

plantation life deadly blows, and many owners lost their fortunes. Only a few Peninsula houses are still in original family hands. Foremost are the massive Shirley, now owned by Mr. and Mrs. Hill Carter, and Sherwood Forest, the long frame house near Williamsburg, to which the self-proclaimed outlaw, John Tyler, retreated from the Presidency in 1845. Grandson Alfred Tyler, a country lawyer, makes his home there with his family.

Life on the plantations inherits the spaciousness of the pre-television age. Today's owners enjoy rusticity without drudgery. Good roads, telephones and electrification have almost made up for the loss of servants. Except to teen-aged sons and daughters, who are drawn away by city lights, plantation life on the Peninsula is a satisfying *mélange* of gardening, cocktails, dinners, swimming parties, shad bakes, party-line gossip, duck-shooting, county politics and Sunday church.

Fox hunting and horse racing have almost disappeared in Tidewater, though still popular in the Piedmont hunt country from Charlottesville northward through Warrenton and Leesburg. A few Peninsula plantation owners commute to offices in nearby cities, but most of them take an old English pride in being "country people" and forswear city ways.

Typical of Peninsula planters are the Carters, who live at Shirley the outdoor family life that Virginians traditionally cherish. Hill Carter, ninth generation of his family to own Shirley, turned down a generous offer of the late John D. Rockefeller, Jr., to endow and preserve the priceless house and its furnishings. Instead Hill Carter preferred to farm it with the encouragement of his wife and three youngsters.

Typifying the newer residents is Bruce Crane Fisher, who inherited Westover from her father, Richard Crane, assistant to Secretary of State Lansing in The Wilson Administration and later minister to Czechoslovakia. Related through her mother to the Bruces of Virginia and Maryland, she chose to wrestle with county welfare problems and work hard for Westover Episcopal Church. In an area where two-thirds of the people are Negroes, she shared her fellow plantation owners' passion to improve schools and increase jobs. At county political meetings and cocktail parties plantation owners have a chronic concern for the need for "clean" industry. In Tidewater Virginia paternalism is still a strong force.

In fact, if one examines it closely, he will conclude that nowhere in America has life changed less in 350 years than here, where English civilization took root in the New World. True, the cut and color of life are different. But the fabric is much the same. In the same Westover bedroom where William Byrd II once danced a daily jig for exercise, the current occupant may vibrate daily on an electric relaxing contraption.

"Drive Slow," says a sign at Berkeley; "This is an Eighteenth Century Road." In the Never-Never land of the Virginia Peninsula, the tides move sluggishly, as they always did, and life goes on despite the cruel changes of time.

Gazing across the James from Jamestown, the first Virginia settlers in 1607 imagined themselves to be in London, looking southward across the Thames. They therefore named the opposite shore Surrey for the English shire bordering London. It has had a provincial quality ever since.

From that day to this, Surry—spelled thus today—and the other Southside counties have remained outside the mainstream of Tidewater Virginia life. Few tidal creeks and rivers opened them up to shipping, with the result that the Southside was cut off from much of the commerce and intellectual life of early Virginia. For hundreds of years it was totally dependent on tobacco, cotton and lumbering. The result is that many enterprising native sons have gone elsewhere to be educated and to find jobs. Today eight of the ten Southside counties that lie closest to the James have a larger population of Negroes than of whites. The landlord-tenant character of the Southside and its dependence on tobacco and peanut prices have bred a Southern conservatism there which is more akin to South Carolina than to Virginia.

For this reason, Southside Virginia preserves more of the paternalistic flavor of pre-Civil War Virginia than any part of the State. Negro field hands work the earth of these "blackbelt" counties. Horses and mules draw farm wagons, and country stores sell food, patent medicine and clothing. Saturday is the week's climax; farm families dress in their best and come to town to shop and socialize. The Baptist and Methodist churches are more dominant here than in the Peninsula counties, where greater numbers of Episcopalians, Presbyterians and Catholics are found.

The waterfront plays a lesser role in Southside life than elsewhere in Tidewater, for its creeks are few and shallow. Hopewell remains a sizeable port, but Smithfield and Suffolk now ship their peanuts, hams and lumber by truck and railway. Boatbuilders, who once thrived in Battery Park and Chuckatuck, today commute to work in Newport News, Portsmouth and Norfolk. Large numbers of young people are migrating to the cities.

Plantation living south of the James has not attracted many newcomers because of the district's inaccessibility. However, a new bridge at Hopewell and another projected at Jamestown will no doubt lead to the area's discovery. Large tracts of adolescent pine trees are owned by pulp companies. Road signs exhort the motorists to "Keep Virginia Green".

Because its environment has changed slowly, Southside has more than its share of early American buildings. Near Smithfield stands St. Luke's Church, believed to have been started about 1632, which would justify its claim to be the oldest Protestant church in America. Outside Norfolk is the brick house that Adam Thoroughgood built in 1634, while opposite Jamestown in Surry County are four pioneer houses: the original frame Chippokes, built in 1642; the story-and-a-half Rolfe-Warren house, which Edward Warren built in 1652 on land that John Rolfe's son inherited from his Indian grandfather, Powhatan; the cross-shaped Bacon's Castle, which Nathaniel Bacon built about 1655; and the frame house that William Edwards built and called Pleasant Point about 1657. Farther up the James, in Prince George County near the colonial port of City Point—now Hopewell—is Merchant's Hope Church, also built about 1657.

Among the plantations that line the south bank of the James are Brandon, a former Harrison house, which is the oldest continuous farming operation in the United States; Claremont, a former Allen plantation, now owned by a Catholic order; Appomattox Manor, the Eppes homestead at Hopewell, which served as General Grant's headquarters for a year during the Civil War; Mount Pleasant, a former Cocke plantation across the James from Jamestown; and Chippokes, onetime Ludwell plantation in the same area.

This corner of Virginia has a towering reputation for the quality of its food. The distinction took root when settlers learned to smoke the meat of hogs allowed to grow wild on Hog Island, a few miles downriver from Jamestown. Another regional speciality is Brunswick stew, a summertime potpourri of meat and garden vegetables, cooked for hours in a huge black cauldron. Outdoor oyster roasts and Brunswick stew parties gave delight to many generations of Tidewater Virginians in the unsophisticated years of the nineteenth and early twentieth centuries. In the glow of autumnal fires which cured the tobacco crop, families gathered to roast ears of corn and to wait for the stew to be ladled out. Gone, alas, are such simple pleasures.

It would be difficult to determine how many famous Southern foods originated in Tidewater Virginia, but they have been many. Salted roe herring is a favorite breakfast dish. Pickled oysters, batter bread, beaten biscuit, fried chicken, deviled crab, fried Norfolk spot and sweet-potato pie are other Tidewater favorites.

Gloucester, the most beautiful of all Tidewater counties, has given its name and character to the whole peninsula between the York and the Rappahannock rivers. No section of the Old Dominion has a more idyllic landscape. Its Mobjack Bay is Gloucester's own little Chesapeake Bay with the sheltered Ware, North and Severn rivers emptying into it. Its small scale reminded English settlers of their own pocket-sized country. The area in the seventeenth century attracted a substantial number of settlers, who staked claims and built waterfront homes ranging from Toddsbury, begun in 1658, to such pillared nineteenth-century mansions as Elmington.

One historian has described Gloucester and York counties as the cultural center of eighteenth-century America. John Clayton, the botanist, lived at Windsor, in Gloucester, and Augustine Warner, a progenitor of Washington and Robert E. Lee as well as of Queen Elizabeth II of England, built Warner Hall there. From Gloucester, Thomas and Armistead Smith entered the College of William and Mary and helped to found Phi Beta Kappa. John Page had the most elaborate house in eighteenth-century America at Rosewell on the York River, where his friend Jefferson is reputed to have worked on a draft of the Declaration of Independence. Gloucester was also the seat of Sir

John Peyton, the only English baronet who came to live permanently in Virginia. Through generations of plantation intermarriage, a well-defined planter class developed by 1700.

The six counties that form the Gloucester peninsula are among the most rustic in Virginia. No railroad penetrates this Eden, and until recently no bridges linked it to the outside world. Small wonder, then, that it preserved the attitudes of colonial days. The great houses have had a continuity of care, and the year-round entertaining on neighboring estates has attracted many newcomers. Retired industrialists and military officers are an important element in the population of Mathews, Middlesex, King and Queen, King William, Caroline and Gloucester. In recent elections, they have swung the vote to the Republican party—an unusual occurrence in rural Tidewater.

Scattered among the great estates are the smaller homes of fishermen-farmers who have resisted city jobs. So long as Virginia's waters continue to yield fish and oysters, these incurable individualists will take their chances on living from the bounty of the sea. Each year the watermen complain that their catch is smaller. Nevertheless, the luxury of being their own boss keeps them at it. After all, factory jobs in these counties are few, and the daily ride to work in Newport News or West Point is a long one.

Church plays a very real part in the life of this region and reveals the inherited class structure. The oldest churches are the beautiful Anglican survivals such as Abingdon and Ware in Gloucester, St. Peter's in New Kent and Christ Church in Middlesex. Many current Episcopal parishioners descend from the First Families buried in their churchyards. Among watermen and farmers, the Methodist Church is the most popular, with the Baptist a close second. Homecoming Sunday each August is a big day in the life of congregations and brings back the younger folk who have strayed to the city. A buffet of ham, chicken and other gastronomic masterpieces is spread on trestle tables. Salvation was never so appealing.

Along the Mattaponi and Pamunkey rivers of the Gloucester peninsula are Indian reservations which bear those names. A handful of old Chief Powhatan's people live in these enclaves, which have been established by the Commonwealth of Virginia. Off the reservation they are hard to recognize as Indians in khakis and blue jeans. Only when they dress in buckskin and feathers (both unauthentic) to present a wild turkey to the Governor are they identifiable as redskins.

Where 9000 Indians roamed Tidewater Virginia in John Smith's day, less than 2500 live there today. Of those who remain, most have intermarried with Negroes. Their scarcity and withdrawal has isolated them until recently from the twentieth century, but automobiles and industrial jobs are beginning to break the barriers. Nowadays they have their own churches, lodges and schools. Gone are the naked savages of 1607.

Even more ingrown and remote than the Gloucester peninsula is the Northern Neck. This is the long and raveled pennant of land which stretches seaward between the Potomac and Rappahannock rivers. Although it lies close to Fredericksburg, not many Virginians are familiar with this remote retreat unless they have been lucky enough to fish and hunt there.

Newcomers are called "come-heres" while natives who have returned to retire are known as "come-back-heres". Author John Dos Passos is a "come-here".

A feudal grandeur envelops the counties that make up the Northern Neck. King Charles II in 1649 granted it to a group of proprietors that included Lord Culpeper. By the marriage of Catherine Culpeper to Thomas, sixth Baron Fairfax, its control passed to him about 1692. The other principal owner was Robert "King" Carter of Corotoman, whose holdings of 300,000 Tidewater acres were second in Virginia only to the Fairfaxes'. Both estates long since have been broken up, but the Northern Neck remains a land of large holdings. A projected scenic parkway from Mount Vernon to Yorktown may soon make it more accessible to sightseers.

The Neck exerted an influence in early Virginia out of proportion to its size. The countryside boasts a wealth of other famous sons. Washington's birthplace, Wakefield, has disappeared, but a similar house has been built by the National Park Service near the site. Nearby is Statford Hall, ancestral home of the Lees, where lived four generations of Virginia's leaders, culminating in the great Robert E. himself. Gunston Hall, home of George Mason, originator of Virginia's early Declaration of Rights, is not far away.

Westmoreland and surrounding counties are full of associations of Washington and Lee. Washington surveyed the area for Lord Fairfax, and the homes of his Ball, Lewis, Fitzhugh and Custis connections are nearby. He served as vestryman of Christ Church, in Alexandria, and often worshipped in Pohick Church, in Fairfax. Lee was a familiar figure to later generations of the same families. With his wife, Mary Randolph Custis, he inherited the pillared Custis mansion, Arlington, overlooking the Potomac at Washington.

Potomac shipping was an important part of Northern Neck commerce until the twentieth century. Being the largest of Virginia's rivers, it provided ample dockage for plantation shipments. The Washingtons of Mount Vernon and the Lees of Stratford were among the planters who shipped tobacco to England and received manufactured goods in return. Alexandria became the Potomac's major port, and in 1800 the site of the new capital of the United States was chosen along its course.

The location of the District of Columbia was a fateful decision for Tidewater Virginia. Northern Virginia land increased in value even though plantation life declined in the industrial nineteenth century. Like other tidal Virginian waters, the Potomac became more valued for its bathing and fisheries than its commerce. Oystering remains an important activity, even today, and oyster wars occasionally flare up between Marylanders on the north shore and Virginians on the south. A chronic irritant is the Mount Vernon Compact of 1785, which gave Maryland jurisdiction up to the low-water mark on the Virginia shore. Maryland patrol boats have accused Virginia tongers in the past of poaching. Hot pursuit and gunfire sometimes ensue.

As the city of Washington grows, this corner of Virginia increasingly feels the fallout of city life. Slowly the Northern Neck is becoming week-end country for Washingtonians. Simplicity is giving way to sophistication. Wild seacoast becomes clustered with cottages. The onetime kingdom of King Carter is becoming a recreation area for the crowded urban corridor that runs northward from Virginia to Boston. Such has been the fate of other Atlantic peninsulas as America grows larger.

No account of Tidewater would be complete without mention of the Eastern Shore, which helps guard the entrance to the Chesapeake.

Though it contains only two counties and 40,000 people, it is aggressively Virginian in spirit. Ever since the early Jamestown colony sent an expedition there to collect fish and salt, Americans have looked to the Eastern Shore for its Chincoteague oysters and cherrystone clams. Bearing the exotic Indian name, Accomack, it was one of the eight original Virginia shires. By the time the colony of Maryland had been chartered by King Charles I in 1632, the Lower Eastern Shore was irretrievably Virginia's.

In fact, the sixty-mile peninsula has become more a part of mainland Virginia than ever since the Chesapeake Bay Bridge Tunnel was completed in 1964, between Norfolk and the lower Shore, at Kiptopeke. Traffic along U.S. 13, the Shore's Main Street, grows as more producers choose this marketway for their perishable goods. Shore farmers send out a constant stream of vans over Route 13, laden with potatoes, seafood, tomatoes, cucumbers, beans, strawberries, jonquils and other perishables. The name Eastern Shore has become synonymous with truck farming.

Time was when the Shore prided itself on its insularity. Until 1953, the Pennsylvania Railroad shuttled freight and passengers through the Shore with the aid of steamer service from Norfolk and Old Point Comfort to Cape Charles. Known to generations as the NipanNen (for New York, Philadelphia and Norfolk), it was the Eastern Shoreman's chief connection with the Outside World. He felt he owned its slim white ships, and he welcomed the sightseers who came to spend holidays in cottages looking out over the Atlantic or the bay.

When declining traffic killed the NipanNen, Eastern Shoremen set up a wail which would be heard up and down the Pennsy's line. Failing to budge the corporate moguls, they persuaded the Commonwealth of Virginia to provide a car ferry service between Kiptopeke and Little Creek, near Norfolk. However, the ferries never achieved the glamour of the NipanNen. Gone were the social gatherings that once took place around the docks as the *S.S. Elisha Lee* was being loaded. No more did burly longshoremen rush to put aboard barrels of oysters, live sea-turtles, boxes of fresh-picked jonquils which once had moved over the NipanNen. For this reason, nobody grieved when the ferries gave way in 1964 to the amazing twenty-one mile bridge-tunnel, which takes the motorist ninety feet beneath the bay channel.

The Eastern Shore has by its remoteness developed a special character. Intermarriage between neighboring families for 300 years has produced an infinity of cousins and a familiar repetition of family names. Youngsters have to a large extent chosen to remain on the Shore rather than to move into Maryland or across the bay. With food and home sites so easy to come by, the Eastern Shore has a strong appeal for those who enjoy the simple life. Like other cults, being a Shoreman arouses either total loyalty or indifference, usually the former.

This provincialism reaches its ultimate on Tangier Island, which sits in Chesapeake Bay between the Northern Neck and the Eastern Shore. Here a populace of 900 inbred watermen looks with suspicion on all visitors. So rigid is the pattern of life that outsiders dare not move to Tangier. Sightseeing vessels take visitors there each summer to marvel at the poke bonnets of this nineteenth-century island awash in a twentieth-century world.

Despite its unmatched locations for the development of ports, Tidewater Virginia witnessed the snail's-pace growth of towns for 300 years. Only in the nineteenth century, after Northern ports had taken the lion's share of America's commerce, did Virginians awaken to their opportunity to make Hampton Roads the threshhold to the mid-Atlantic states.

The Virginia Company of London had tried in Virginia's early years to encourage settlers to build towns. They named its first sub-divisions James City, Charles City and Elizabeth City, and urged settlers to plant close together. However, the demands of tobacco and the abundance of land encouraged a decentralized economy. The ports that developed in Virginia's first 200 years—Jamestown, York, Tyndall's Point in Gloucester—were generally small harbors which could not accommodate the larger ships that were later built in the age of steam.

The growth of Virginia's ports was also delayed by bitter rivalry between Tidewater and western Virginia in the nineteenth century. Pioneers who lived beyond the mountains (now Southwest Virginia, West Virginia and Kentucky) wanted Virginia's government to sub-sidize a railroad which would funnel their produce into Richmond and Norfolk, as the Baltimore and Ohio Railway was doing in Baltimore. However, the old-fashioned free-enterprise Tidewater sentiment was against government subsidy. By the time Virginia awoke to its mistaken choice of canals over rails, the industrialization of the North was well established.

Virginia's port cities were far behind New York and Philadelphia by the time Collis Potter Huntington, the California empire-builder, chose Newport News in 1883 as the eastern terminus of the Chesapeake and Ohio Railway. The Norfolk and Western in 1876 selected Norfolk as its Atlantic port, and the Virginian followed in 1909. Thus, belatedly, the lower Chesapeake, whose harbor had prompted England's decision to settle Virginia in the first place, at last began to realize its destiny. In 1917 the United States Navy chose Hampton Roads as the base of its Atlantic fleet. This basin is now one of the world's busiest waterways, with a ring of bridges and tunnels connecting Norfolk, Portsmouth, Newport News, Hampton and the Eastern Shore.

The fall-line towns which mark the northern perimeter of Tidewater have also grown, though they have lost their primacy as ports to Hampton Roads. Richmond has grown steadily since the capital was moved there from Williamsburg in 1780, to spare the seat of government from possible bombardment by British men-of-war. Its golden age was the early nineteenth century, when Chief Justice John Marshall was its first citizen and such men as George Wythe, Edmund Randolph, Henry Clay, James Monroe and John Tyler frequented Capitol Square. That early Richmond was a neo-classical village on the hills overlooking the falls of the James, with the tobacco-barge canal running through its center. Edgar Allan Poe spent his young manhood here, and Lafayette, Thackeray and Dickens were celebrated visitors.

Despite its burning in the Civil War, much of the older Richmond survives. In common with the other fall-line settlements, the city has preserved more of the tone of early Tidewater than have the ports of Hampton Roads. It exhibits a stubborn provincialism that pleases residents but annoys newcomers. Norfolkians scoffingly call it "The Holy City" and boast of their faster progress. However, the diehard Richmonder is unashamedly pleased with his world as it was. A similar traditionalism survives in Petersburg, Fredericksburg and Alexandria.

Two alien and diverse cultures met in Tidewater to form the character of Virginia. One was the Anglo-Saxon emigration which began in 1606 from London and which continued for more than 200 years. The other was the culture of Africa, whose slaves built the tobacco and cotton fortunes of the Tidewater gentry beginning in 1620. Both loom large in the consciousness of Virginia today.

The English character sticks out all over. It is there in the names of ancient counties and sleepy towns. It is seen in fine Georgian houses, boxwood gardens, and wind-swept clusters of jonquils blooming in spring under the limbs of ancient oaks. It is inherent in the Virginian's simplicity and his fondness for old things, in his Old Testament idealism, in his deeprootedness in his land and his family. Like his English forefathers, he is a practical man who shuns extremes, is skeptical of political solutions and is embarrassed by display of emotion or religiosity. His thought processes are colored by an eighteenth-century paternalism that seeks consensus through courtesy and compromise.

But the one unmistakable mark of the Tidewater Virginian is his accent. Over the centuries it has lost the precision of England and taken on the languor of Negro speech. "Huntin'" and "fishin'" are not mere words but a philosophy of life. "Fourth" comes out as "fo'th", and "park" as "pauk". The vowel "i" is sometimes clouded so that "Tidewater" sounds like "Tahdwatuh". The most characteristic local pronunciation is the "ou" in "house" and "out". On a Tidewater tongue it becomes a sound between "oo" and "ow". Virginians believe it a Scottish inheritance, but Scotsmen seem in no haste to claim it.

Another Tidewater locution which is fast disappearing is the insertion of a "y" sound in words like "garden" and "car". They emerge as "gyarden" and "cyar". One Virginia lady recently announced her intention to go to New York to hear "Cyarmen" and to see the "Ballet Russe de Monte Cyarlo". This and the broad "a" (a clearly English inheritance) are still heard in the speech of Garden Club ladies and old-school Episcopal ministers, but they are dying out.

Rural Tidewater Negroes are the best conservators of archaic speech. They use such words as "feisty" (for "quarrelsome") and "chauncified" (for "stuck up"), and pronounce "aunt" and "haunt" as "ant" and "hant". They will describe a day as "right nice" and a distance as "near 'bout as far". They display positive genius in stretching words into new shapes. Bothersome youngsters are "trundle-bed trash", and dolts "cymling heads". Nouns become verbs, as in "I don't

26

fault you for that". In reproof, one Negro matron tells another: "Yo mouth ain' no prayer book".

The influence of the two races on each other in Tidewater Virginia has been close and amicable. Planters' children were raised by Negro "aunts". House servants attended church with their masters and often were buried in family graveyards. The proprietary attitude of Negroes toward their owner's family survived long after Emancipation. "Mind yo' manners," a Negro mammy scolded her young white charges a few years ago in Richmond's Monroe Park. "Manners git you whar money won't."

Tidewater's Negroes typify the rock-ribbed fundamentalism which enveloped the nineteenth-century South. Born to a life of labor, they took hope from the Bible's promise of heaven. The spirituals and jubilee songs which emerged from the slave huts reveal their very souls. The paternalism of the whites and the religion of the blacks did much to lighten the darkness of the South's long night of slavery.

The marshes and flatlands of Tidewater support a myriad plant and animal life. It ranges from the Cape Henry's Spanish moss and live-oaks to the mountain laurels which spill down from the Appalachians. Because the Gulf Stream buffers the Atlantic winds a few miles off Virginia's coast, Tidewater enjoys mild winters and normally generous rainfall. Plants, trees and birds of semi-tropical variety abound in fields and forests.

The loblolly pine is the giant of the landscape. What the palm is to Florida and the spruce to New England, this gaunt tree is to the Chesapeake region. It towers like a king over the forests, sheltering hardwoods and smaller scrub pines in its shade. Many a Virginia landowner lives comfortably from the sale of fast-growing pines to feed voracious paper mills. Taller specimens are used for masts. English shipyards imported them for just this purpose in Virginia's first years.

A wealth of dogwood enamels Tidewater with porcelain whiteness each April. Many other plants contribute to spring's symphony: the dainty shadblow, the white-flowering plum, the magenta Judas-tree and the bright yellow Scotch broom whose seed is said to have come from Scotland in forage for British cavalry horses in the Revolution. Tropical brilliance radiates from festoons of purple wistaria and of

27

yellow Carolina jasmine, both of which climb over trees and buildings. Later in summer, the spiky yucca or Spanish sword sends up a showy stalk of white flowers that suggests the cactus of the Southwest. Magnolia trees recall the heavy sentimentalism of the South "before the War".

Repeated planting of tobacco impoverished Tidewater's soil in the eighteenth century, and many planters moved to new lands. However, crop rotation and fertilization have restored soil productiveness. The pressing farm problem today is labor supply.

The animals and birds of the region, which lived comfortably on the agricultural economy, are finding life more difficult as Tidewater industrializes. The decline in catches of fish, crabs and oysters has led to State controls. The wild-game population has suffered less. Virginia white-tailed deer are abundant in many areas. Ducks, geese, rabbits, squirrels and partridges provide sport for huntsmen from neighboring states. The red fox has been hunted almost to extinction, which accounts for the decline in fox-hunting in Tidewater. Not so the dull-witted opossum and skunk, which frequently fall victims of automobiles on rural highways.

Tidewater's richest wild-life legacy is its birds. Along the swamps fly bald eagles whose nests can be seen high up in waterfront trees. Feeding largely on fish, these magnificent predators have felt the damage wrought to sea-life by pollution. Rare cranes and ospreys also live along these waterways, while woods and meadows all summer long are enraptured with the cadenzas of mockingbirds. Many birds fly south from northern climes to winter in the Chesapeake region.

Of all Tidewater regions, the Dismal Swamp provides the wildest variety of wild life. This humid forest extends southward across the North Carolina line from the city of Chesapeake. Its thick and impenetrable depths are haunted with mystery. They also shelter black bears, wildcats and other predators which have been hunted to extinction elsewhere in the eastern United States.

Virginians, who are used to living among the landmarks and debris of three and a half centuries, develop a curious unawareness of time. A man who has seen the friends of his youth grow old along with him continues to think of them as the young men he once knew. So it is with a born-and-bred resident of Tidewater. Its history is a contemporary landscape which he cannot divide into "old" and "new".

The avalanche of events which has swept over Tidewater since 1607 therefore seems a living and continuing present to the dyed-in-the-wool Virginian. If he himself has not witnessed all of it, at least he has heard so much about it that it seems to have been a part of his experience.

But the pulse of Tidewater has begun to beat at a quickened rate. Two world wars have changed its metabolism. Its face, too, has altered more in the fifty years since the introduction of the automobile than in the whole 300 years before it. Rivers have ceased to be channels of communication. Expressways have wakened rural Virginia from a long lethargy. Cities have grown to dominate the countryside for miles around. Bridges and tunnels have removed barriers which for 300 years discouraged commerce and industry.

Aided by modern transport, the armed forces have ringed Hampton Roads with defenses. Factories have moved in, pulling farm dwellers to the cities. In a pattern familiar to the North a century earlier, Tidewater has begun to feel the urbanization of its agricultural life.

With industry has come a revolution in relations between whites and Negroes. In the last ten years Tidewater has seen the peaceful integration of its schools, even in the counties where Negroes outnumber whites. This was the final blow to paternalism. Like all social changes, it sacrificed one ideal for another: in this case, the equalitarian ethos of the machine age is replacing the older concept of political and social leadership by an educated élite. The long ascendancy of White Anglo-Saxon Protestants which produced Virginia's eighteenth-century golden age is giving way to a pluralistic conception of the Great Society.

In this transitional age Tidewater Virginia is a paradoxical paradise, hovering between present and past.

You can see it on a hot August afternoon in Surry Courthouse, where farmers in trucks and wagons come to buy and sell, right beneath the CAB flyway of jet planes which sweep at 400 miles an hour between Norfolk and Washington.

You can see it on the Poquoson River, where oystermen grapple with crude tongs just offshore of the NASA's vast space laboratories.

29

You can see it on the Eastern Shore, where farmhands dig potatoes under the shadow of the Wallops Island missile range.

You can sense it at Arlington plantation house, from which Lee once gazed across the Potomac to Washington amid the shambles of Reconstruction. Those were the darkest days in Virginia's long history.

You can hear it in Richmond's Capitol Square, where America's oldest legislative assembly debates in Jefferson's Capitol, encircled by skyscrapers.

The older order changes, and Tidewater Virginia accepts the change.

THE PLATES

JAMES FORT

The first English settlers to plant England's flag successfully on American soil landed in Virginia on May 13, 1607. There, while Captain Christopher Newport and his thirty-nine crewmen explored the James River and its tributaries, the 104 settlers built a triangular palisade and named it King James His Town, or as later generations knew it, Jamestown.

Alas, the fort long since fell into disuse and collapsed. Even the low-lying sandspit on which it stood has washed away. Despite their best efforts, archeologists cannot firmly identify the location of the original James Fort, with its "fine row" of houses, its church, its "cape merchant's" storehouse and its guardhouse and *corps du garde*. Jamestown does retain, however, the stout brick tower of the church built 1639. It is believed to be on the site of the wooden church where the first representative legislative assembly in the New World met in 1619. And nearby are the remains of the statehouses from which Virginia was governed until the colonial capital was moved to Middle Plantation in 1699.

The Federal and State governments have re-created many visions of early Jamestown. In the Park Service's Visitor Center, the ninety-two-year history of the first capital is told in small-scale dioramas, amplified by artifacts recovered from the 1500 swampy acres of Jamestown. And at the adjoining Glasshouse Point, the Commonwealth of Virginia has reconstructed the three ships, the fort and other scenes of the first settlement. Like Jamestown itself, Jamestown Festival Park is open all year.

Inside the reconstructed James Fort in the park, visitors may sense the remote and simple life of John Smith and his fellow settlers. A moat surrounds the spiked timber walls. Guns protect the entrance and the bulwarks. Inside the simple thatched houses, built of wattle-and-daub, some of the chores of John Smith's day are repeated for a grateful posterity.

32

SAINT LUKE'S CHURCH

The cultural center of colonial Virginia lay between the James River and the Potomac River, extending inland from Chesapeake Bay to the fall of the rivers, about fifty miles away. Most of the well-known houses and churches of the early Old Dominion lie within this area. It is therefore unexpected to find Virginia's oldest surviving church outside this magic circle. Saint Luke's Church is believed to have been undertaken beginning in 1632, a mere twenty-five years after Virginia was settled. Whatever its precise date, Saint Luke's is assuredly the oldest standing church in the nation and a monument to the faith of settlers who claimed their lands in Warrasquyoake Shire—later changed to Isle of Wight County—on the south side of the James River.

Used for more than 300 years for Episcopal worship, Saint Luke's is the only original Gothic church still standing in America. It retains its original brick walls with thick quoins, traceried windows, stepped gables to decorate its roofline and buttresses to support the weight of its medieval-style roof. "In many respects", declares architectural historian Thomas E. Tallmadge, "it is the most precious building in America."

Inside the church, the arrangement is typical of the few surviving English churches which date back to the reign of King James I. The rood screen is the first to be restored in any seventeenth-century church in America. The communion table and chairs are among the rare examples of the earliest American craftsmen. The seventeenth-century silver baptismal basin is set in a hewn log font, carefully shaped. In such other details as its silver wine ewers for communion services, its "breeches" bible and its high pulpit, Saint Luke's takes us back to the England of Archbishop Laud and of Shakespeare. Saved and endowed for posterity by the St. Luke's Foundation, the church is open to the public throughout the year.

34

ADAM THOROUGHGOOD HOUSE

Probably the oldest brick dwelling in North America is the Adam Thorough-good House, which was built in Princess Anne County between 1636 and 1640 by an early planter who had come to Virginia from England as an indentured servant. Adam Thoroughgood built his stout house in the style of medieval England. Its steep roof rises between wide triangular chimneys. Windows are few and small, their diamond panes providing little light inside. Cooking was done on spits and griddles in the wide fireplaces at each end of the house.

Thoroughgood was typical of the young Englishmen, usually poor, who settled early Virginia. Through hard work and careful husbandry, he amassed substantial land and other property. Not until nearly a hundred years later did Virginia attain the great plantation society of its Golden Age, based on the cheap labor of slavery. In Adam Thoroughgood's day, however, each planter was his own overseer—and sometimes his best field hand.

While it lacks the beauty of the more graceful houses of a later day, Adam Thoroughgood's home is a rare example of early Virginia craftmanship. No other house of so early a date is so well preserved. Maintained by the city of Norfolk with an attractive seventeenth-century garden restored by the Garden Club of Virginia, it is one of Virginia's prides.

36

THE WREN BUILDING, COLLEGE OF WILLIAM AND MARY

The building of The College of William and Mary at the end of the seventeenth century led to the removal of Virginia's capital from medieval Jamestown to the newly laid out village of Williamsburg. The little town was the center of Virginia's eighteenth-century flowering of tobacco wealth and political genius, with its power focused in the Capitol, where the Royal Governor held sway, and the College, where the Reverend James Blair held the reigns of power tightly as president for more than fifty years. During these exciting years, Virginia—the largest and most populous of England's New World colonies—differed increasingly from the Mother Country in her interest. The political liberalism of John Locke, of Jean Jacques Rousseau and of the Enlightenment found friendly soil among skeptical Virginians. The College became a hotbed of new thought and the concept that man was born with certain natural rights took vigorous root. Ideas of liberty, fraternity and equality flourished.

Chartered in 1693, the College opened a few years later in a handsome brick structure in the style of Sir Christopher Wren. Its grammar school and college students attended classes and went to Anglican chapel on its main floor, using the dormer floor for bedrooms. They included such unusual young men as Thomas Jefferson, James Monroe, Benjamin Harrison and John Tyler. Other remarkable men served on its faculty. "I know of no place in the world," wrote Jefferson in 1788, "while the present professors remain, where I would so soon place a son."

During the twentieth-century renaissance of the College and the rest of eighteenth-century Williamsburg, the Wren Building has been restored to its original condition. The handsome face which it presents to Duke of Gloucester Street is unchanged, except for the grace of age, since Jefferson's day.

38

DUKE OF GLOUCESTER STREET

Franklin D. Roosevelt called it "the most historic avenue in all America". Certainly, Williamsburg's Duke of Gloucester Street has witnessed more vital events in the life of America than any other one-mile thoroughfare in the nation. From the College of William and Mary at one end to the Capitol at the other, it evokes memories of eighty years—from 1699 to 1779—when Williamsburg was capital of the colony of Virginia.

A typical segment of houses along the street is shown here, with Burdett's Ordinary in the foreground. These structures are close to the Capitol, on the north side of the street, where rooms and meals for visiting burgesses and councilors were much in demand. At the sign of Edinburgh Castle, John Burdett kept his tavern and welcomed legislators and other patrons. On his death, an inventory of his effects listed "crackt" plates, "1 old Fiddle", "1 billiard table with sticks, balls, etc.", "11 pr. dice", and "a Quantity of choice old Madeira Wine, and old Barbados Rum".

Adjoining the ordinary is the John Crump House, which in turn is followed by the site of Robert Nicolson, who conducted a tailor shop and store there. The next structure visible is the Pasteur-Galt Apothecary Shop, whose sign portrays the mortar and pestle of that trade, and then the residence of Joseph Scrivener, who from 1762 until 1772 conducted a store and sold such things as West India goods, oriental wares and Portuguese wine.

The plan for Williamsburg was devised by Governor Francis Nicholson, with the spacious influence of the Italian Renaissance clearly evident. Half-acre lots were laid off, and a uniform setback was prescribed for town houses to insure a pleasant appearance. Duke of Gloucester Street was the principal street, being bisected about midway by the Palace Green. Between the town's four major sites—the College, Capitol, Church and Governor's Palace—were homes and shops of pleasing appearance. Such was the setting for historic events.

THE GOVERNOR'S PALACE

Many visitors to Williamsburg regard the Governor's Palace as the epitome of that town's charm. Its dramatic setting at the end of Palace Green proclaims the importance of the English monarch's representative in Virginia, the oldest and largest of Great Britain's colonies in the New World. Furthermore, the handsome detail of the enclosure, with its steep central house and flanking offices and gardens, is appropriate to the Palace's role as erstwhile social center of Virginia life—the Buckingham Palace of eighteenth-century Williamsburg.

The creation of a seat for the Royal Governor began in 1706. The Assembly set aside £3000, and Henry Cary, who had supervised the building of the Capitol, was given charge. Artisans who could do such refined work were few in Virginia, and the project was not completed until about 1720, during the administration of Governor Alexander Spotswood. What had been intended as a house was ironically dubbed "Palace" by the taxpayers, who resented the added levies but who came to take pride in the resulting building.

The Palace served both as a home and an office. The main building is similar to English country houses built during the reign of the first two Georges, and it has been credited as the first Georgian house built in America. To heighten its official look, the forecourt has castellated walls, and the building is topped by a cupola, or "lantern" as it was first called, above a balustraded roof. On the monarch's birthday and other special occasions, the lantern was lighted.

The Palace was repaired in 1751, and the interior is thought to have been remodeled. It was probably then that the ballroom and supper room were added at the rear of the house, forming the stem of a T. These handsome rooms made possible larger entertainments appropriate to a growing colony.

42

STRATFORD HALL

On 1200 remote acres in Westmoreland County, on Virginia's proud Northern Neck, stands Stratford Hall, seat of the famous Lee family. Built by Thomas Lee, the first native-born Virginian to be governor of the colony, Stratford was the home of four remarkable generations of Lees, culminating in the heroic Robert E. Lee of Civil War fame.

Thomas Lee's famous sons Richard Henry Lee and Francis Lightfoot Lee were born at Stratford, became statesmen of the Revolution and were the only brothers who signed the Declaration of Independence. And Thomas Lee's great nephew, Henry "Lighthorse Harry" Lee, was the father of the Confederate hero, who was born in the Mother's Room of the huge H-shaped house near the Potomac.

During the years 1725 to 1830 when the Lees made Stratford famous, the plantation amply supported a large and demanding family. Now preserved by the Robert E. Lee Memorial Foundation, it is open throughout the year to the public. The plantation still grows corn, barley and hay, and its restored mill grinds flour and meal. Hams are cured over hickory smoke in the smokehouse, and other crafts of the self-sufficient planter are exhibited for the visitor. The manor house and its four dependencies have been restored as one of the most interesting survivals extant of an unusual architectural design.

Perhaps no family in America exerted greater influence on the direction of early political affairs than did the Lees. Stratford Hall gives a fascinating insight into their lives and times.

44

SHIRLEY PLANTATION

No early Virginia county enjoyed a more convivial society than Charles City, which lies on the north side of the James midway between Williamsburg and Richmond. There lived the Hills and the Carters at Shirley, the Harrisons at Berkeley, the Byrds at Westover, the Tylers at Greenway and many another hospitable family. Of the houses, none has greater architectural interest than Shirley, which to an amazing extent preserves its original materials, colors and furnishings.

Records mention Shirley as early as 1611, and the estate was settled in 1613. In 1660 the Hill family acquired the plantation, and they and the intermarried Carters have owned and occupied it ever since. The present owners, Mr. and Mrs. Hill Carter, open the house and its gardens to the public. Washington and Jefferson were guests in the house, which was built beginning in 1723 by the third Edward Hill. His daughter Elizabeth married John Carter, son of the famous "King" Carter, who was regarded in his time as the wealthiest Virginian. The house was completed in 1770, equipped with splendid paneling, carved interior decorations and a graceful three-story staircase. Among the famous people to be born in the house was Ann Hill Carter, who married General Henry "Lighthouse Harry" Lee of Revolutionary fame. They were the parents of Robert E. Lee, who received part of his schooling at Shirley.

The plantation no longer grows tobacco; its cultivation is most successful today in the warmer counties south of the James River. However, it continues to grow corn, barley, oats, wheat, cattle and sheep, as in the days of yore. Interesting outbuildings and barns, built of brick in the typical Flemish bond pattern of the eighteenth century, surround this jewel of the early American builder's art.

46

WAKEFIELD PLANTATION

The Father of His Country was born in 1732 at Wakefield Plantation in Westmoreland County. The house was built between 1723 and 1725 for Augustine Washington and fronted on Pope's Creek, about thirty-eight miles east of Fredericksburg. When young Washington was three years old, his father moved his family to the Hunting Creek plantation now known as Mount Vernon. Wakefield was burned accidentally during the Revolutionary War, but in the 1930's the home site and 394 surrounding acres were acquired by the National Park Service. There in 1932 it erected a house typical of the period of Washington's birth. However, it is not intended as a reconstruction of the original, about which little is known. The Wakefield National Memorial Association initiated and participated in the project.

Near the front door of the house are an old hackberry tree, fig trees, herbs and flowers which may derive from the gardens of the Washington era. The 100-year-old boxwood was brought from the home of Sarah Tayloe Washington, a daughter of the last owner of the birthplace home. In the garden are found only flowers and shrubs common to Virginia gardens. A rebuilt frame kitchen near the house displays artifacts recovered by archeologists in their search for the original house and its survivals.

The first Washington ancestor of our first President came to Virginia in 1656. Three generations of the family were active in the colony's life before George's birth. His great-grandfather, the emigrant John Washington, settled in Westmoreland. John's son, Lawrence, held the highest political offices of the county. And Lawrence's son Augustine, George Washington's father, increased the family's estates and political influence. It was Augustine Washington who built the first Wakefield. There his second wife, Mary Ball, on February 22, 1732, bore him the son who was to become the most famous American of all time.

Wakefield is open to visitors throughout the year.

48

BERKELEY PLANTATION

The principal seat of the Harrison family in Virginia is Berkeley, built in 1726 by the fourth Benjamin Harrison, father of a son by the same name who was a delegate to the Continental Congress, signed the Declaration of Independence and was three times governor of Virginia. This eminent Revolutionary figure was a friend of George Washington, who often visited Berkeley, as did every other President until Lincoln. President William Henry Harrison, who was born at Berkeley and moved to the Northwest Territory, returned there to write his inaugural address. Yet another Harrison to serve as President was Benjamin, son of William Henry, who occasionally visited his ancestral home and enjoyed its unmatched view of the James across lowland meadows fringed with willow trees.

Perhaps no Virginia plantation has a longer history of importance. The Berkeley grant was made by King James I in 1619 to a company of English settlers, who arrived on December 4 of that year. Jamestown had been settled only twelve years, and Indians were a constant threat. Berkeley's investors instructed their settlers that "The day of our ships' arrival . . . shall be yearly and perpetually kept as a day of Thanksgiving", giving rise to the annual observance of Thanksgiving each December until the Indian massacre in 1622 wiped out many lives; it was thereafter observed in March. When the present plantation house was built 104 years later, Harrison's Landing was one of the chief plantation tobacco ports on the river.

In the Revolution, Berkeley was plundered by British troops under Benedict Arnold. In the Civil War, it was headquarters for General George B. McClellan after the Battle of Malvern Hill. While quartered there with McClellan's command in 1862, a Union general composed the military bugle call known as "Taps", or "Lights Out". In the postwar desolation, Berkeley declined but was later acquired and restored by loving owners. It is open to the public.

BRUTON PARISH CHURCH

Religious belief and worship played a central part in the life of early Virginia. In the counties and towns of Tidewater, a handsome brick church usually stood near the center of population, prepared to serve all classes and conditions of early Virginia. Such a church is Bruton Parish, in Williamsburg, which continues to serve a growing congregation in the midst of the restored town.

Built from 1711 to 1715, the present church is actually the third to serve Middle Plantation and its outgrowth. The Parish was formed in 1674 by the merger of two earlier parishes, one of which is believed to have had a small church near Queen's Creek prior to that date. What is thought to be the second church was completed in 1683 near the present church. It proved inadequate when Williamsburg became the capital, and was replaced by the present structure.

Because it was the "court church", Bruton was built to a scale and a style not previously achieved in the colony. A pew was designated for the governor and his twelve councilors, while transept pews were reserved for burgesses during annual sessions of the General Assembly. Later, separate balconies were built for students at the College and for slaves.

Because of the union of church and state, office holders were obliged to conform to the Established Church. The rector of Bruton during the eighteenth century usually served as chaplain to the House of Burgesses and often simultaneously as president of the College. In turn, the Governor and other colonial officials took part in the services at Bruton by reading the lessons.

After Williamsburg ceased to be Virginia's capital, Bruton's congregation dwindled and its interior was divided into church and Sunday school. However, the structure was returned to its original appearance in a series of restorations begun in 1905–1907 by the Reverend William Archer Rutherfoord Goodwin, who later interested John D. Rockefeller, Jr. in restoring the entire town. The church remains open to visitors and worshipers through the year.

THE WILLIAMSBURG CAPITOL

When Jamestown's fourth Statehouse burned in 1698, members of the General Assembly decided to move Virginia's capital from the marshy peninsula on the James to a more central location. They chose Middle Plantation, which was so called because it lay halfway between the major ports of Jamestown and Yorktown, on the peninsula formed by the James and York rivers. They then renamed the town Williamsburg for the king.

While the legislators made temporary use of the College of William and Mary, a handsome Capitol was built at the east end of Duke of Gloucester Street, a mile away. On this site the General Assembly met each year from 1704 to 1780, taking a leading part in formulating the ideal of American independence which led to the Revolution, 1776–1783. Here George Washington received the thanks of fellow burgesses for his role in the French and Indian War. Patrick Henry thundered against the Stamp Act in the Burgesses' chamber, and George Mason introduced his Declaration of Rights there.

The unusual building consists of two wings joined in a U shape. The principal chamber of one was for meetings of the Burgesses, while the other was the courtroom of the General Court, whose members in the colony's innocent early years were also members of the Governor's Council. This élite body was a sort of House of Lords, whose members were appointed by the King on recommendation of the Governor. Membership usually went to elder members of the Tidewater aristocracy. Such families as the Carters, Lees, Randolphs, Burwells and Pages usually had a member thereon during the eighty years when Williamsburg was capital of Virginia's vast empire, which then included the present Kentucky and West Virginia and extended northward to the Great Lakes.

The present Capitol was reconstructed and is exhibited by Colonial Williamsburg.

54

GOVERNOR'S PALACE GARDENS

The splendor of the Governor's Palace in Williamsburg is enhanced by its gardens. Likened to those at Hampton Court and other English mansions, they take the stroller through a succession of views and prospects which blend the artistry of architect, horticulturist and sculptor.

The Palace and its gardens show the influence of Dutch design, for it was built close upon the reign of William III, who was born and reared in the Netherlands. The Dutch were masters of landscape beautification and artfully expanded many of the principles of Italian Renaissance design in laying out their grounds.

Notable for their classical orderliness, the palace gardens in a series of squares and rectangles lead the stroller from one delight to another. Some areas are for pure pleasure, like the wide central garden walk with its flanking flower borders, pleached beech arbors and grassed courtyards. Adroitly obscured from view by plantings are such service areas as the smokehouse, laundry, wellhead and salthouse.

This scene shows the rear of the Palace during tulip season in May. Projecting from the central structure is the ballroom wing, adjoining which stand the "twelve apostles", as the cylindrical yaupons were called. Walkways made of crushed oyster shell were generally edged in dwarf boxwood, with a graceful bench or leaden urn alternating occasionally with shubbery. In one rectangle is a holly maze, patterned after that at Hampton Court. A tree-shaded mount protects the icehouse. To the west of the Palace, a canal and terraced gardens provided other pleasing prospects for the Governor and his family.

The influence of the Palace's architecture and gardens was strongly felt in the plantations that were built subsequently in Virginia's "golden age" of planter life.

THE SWAN TAVERN

No lovelier town existed in early Virginia than York, later called Yorktown, on the cliffs overlooking the brilliant river of the same name. The town was created by the Virginia House of Burgesses in 1691—although much tobacco had already been shipped from docks built in the early years of the colony to serve the prosperous York River plantations. It helped to concentrate the tobacco trade in one place and to reduce the calls at separate plantation ports which ships had previously been required to make.

Several steep streets led down from Yorktown's heights to its dock street and warehouses. Paralleling the river, along the heights, sat the homes of principal families such as the Nelsons, Reads, Digges, Somerwells and Sessions, all dating from the eighteenth century or earlier. Near the west end of the street is Swan Tavern, now reconstructed by the Park Service. Within a block of Main Street are Grace Episcopal Church, first built in 1697, and the Yorktown Victory Monument, which was erected by the United States government a hundred years after Washington's great victory, in 1881.

Swan Tavern was a typical public house of the eighteenth century, serving ale, wines, rum and simple fare. Travelers could also lodge there and have their servants and horses rested and provisioned in outbuildings to the rear. No doubt the bartender sang out the familiar warning to patrons before closing time: "Mind your P's and Q's" (pints and quarts).

Though smaller than in colonial days, Yorktown is still an active community. It is today part of a historic triangle, which starts at Jamestown, reaches its apex at Williamsburg and concludes at Yorktown, where colonial America came of age.

58

WESTOVER PLANTATION

The most polished gentleman and scholar in pre-Jeffersonian Virginia was William Byrd II, whose father had come to Virginia to claim lands he inherited and to trade in furs with the Indians of Virginia's western territory. It was the son who built the present house, beginning about 1730, at Westover on the James, beneath a grove of huge trees in Charles City County.

In some respects, Westover is the best-proportioned of the colonial mansions. Its steep roof, well-spaced windows and handsome carved doorways have unusual visual appeal. Its wings, built later than the central house, give it a long and balanced façade.

Much of the interest of the house lies in the fascinating personality of the builder, known as the "black swan of Westover", and his son William Byrd III, who dissipated the family's estates at the gambling table. The house passed to another family in 1814. It remains privately owned, though its handsome gardens are open to the public.

The history of Westover was well documented by William Byrd II in his shorthand private diary, which was transcribed and published only in the twentieth century. They reveal their author to have been a man of unusual literary skill, wit, knowledge and *joie de vivre*. He kept up a steady correspondence with English friends, and he was a careful observer of Indian life and of the flora and fauna of North America.

A collateral branch of the Byrd family produced Harry Flood Byrd, who was Virginia's youngest twentieth-century governor and served thereafter as United States Senator.

60

BRANDON PLANTATION

Among the handsomest trees and boxwood to be seen in eastern America are those at Brandon Plantation, on the upper James River in Prince George County. The house looks across formal gardens to the north shore of the river, once alive with tobacco ships but now used chiefly by pleasure boats. The land was patented in 1617 and thus is one of the oldest occupied sites in Virginia. Captain John Martin, its first owner, was a stormy figure in the colony's political and social life. The land was long known as "Martin's Brandon".

In 1720 it was purchased by Nathaniel Harrison, a descendant of the first Benjamin Harrison, who patented Wakefield Plantation in nearby Surry County as early as 1635. This early settler was the first of the long line of Harrisons who also built Berkeley Plantation in Charles City County, across the river from Wakefield and Brandon. The present Brandon house was built about 1770 and consists of a handsome central structure with one-story wings, terminating in flanking two-story units.

Like many of the James River houses, Brandon was visited by British troops during the Revolution. The British General Phillips landed at its dock on May 7, 1781.

Brandon's tilled fields and herds of cattle and sheep make it probably the oldest continuous farming operation in Virginia. Its dairy herd is famed today, and its fields still produce fine crops of grain and hay. Gardens and grounds are open to the public throughout the year.

RALEIGH TAVERN

Eighteenth-century Williamsburg led a double life. Most of the year it was a quiet village of some 1800 people. Its merchants and shopkeepers received goods from England, sold them to Virginians and were paid in tobacco notes or goods —seldom in cash. But for a few weeks each spring the town expanded to a population of 4000 or 5000. Travelers arriving at its taverns had to sleep three or four to a bed for lack of space. Horses raced, and balls were given nightly to entertain the visitors. This was Publick Times, the annual gathering of law-makers, judges and lawyers.

One of the popular centers with visitors was Raleigh Tavern, operated by Anthony Hay. Located between the Capitol and the Governor's Palace, it drew its clientele from the most distinguished families of the colony. In 1775, the Williamsburg Volunteers met there in honor of Peyton Randolph's return from presiding over the Continental Congress in Philadelphia. Next year, citizens gave a dinner honoring Patrick Henry. The signing of the Treaty of Paris, in 1783, ending the Revolution was celebrated there with a triumphal parade and dinner.

The Raleigh's entrance was crowned with a leaden bust of Sir Walter Raleigh over the doorway. On the main floor were the spacious Apollo Room, parlor, bar and other public rooms. Upstairs were bedrooms, sparsely furnished, for the men who came from the far corners of the colony to make Virginia's laws. Shown here is the arrival of a family from rural Virginia, equipped with brass-studded leather trunk and other luggage.

Raleigh Tavern is today an exhibition building of Colonial Williamsburg.

TAPROOM OF RALEIGH TAVERN

The most famous of Williamsburg's many taverns was the Raleigh. This was because the Virginia burgesses adjourned there in 1769 to draw up a boycott of British goods when Governor Lord Botetourt dissolved the Assembly because of its protest against the British Revenue Act. The Raleigh was the scene of another "rump Assembly" in 1774 after news reached Virginia that Britain had ordered Boston's port closed.

The tavern vied with others near the Capitol for the patronage of legislators. Nearby, at different times during the eighteenth century, were Chowning's Tavern, Market Square Tavern, Brick House Tavern, Burdett's Ordinary and Christiana Campbell's. Because of its unusual history, the Raleigh has left the fullest record. Balls were held in its Apollo Room, and the returning Marquis de Lafayette was welcomed at a memorable banquet there in 1824, attended by John Marshall, John C. Calhoun and many others. After an evening there in 1763, a student named Thomas Jefferson wrote his friend John Page: "Last night, as merry as agreeable company and dancing with Belinda in the Apollo could make me, I never could have thought the succeeding Sun would have seen me so wretched."

The room shown here is the taproom, with its bar and tables for loungers. Here townsmen and visitors met over a pint of ale, a glass of port or Madeira or a cup of hot rum punch. Here land sales were negotiated, politics were talked and news dispatches were read from the *Virginia Gazette* and papers arriving by post rider from the north. Posted on tavern doors were ads and public notices.

The Raleigh burned in December 1859, a few months after the "fair and accomplished ladies of Williamsburg" held a banquet for alumni of the College of William and Mary, including former President John Tyler. The tavern was reconstructed by Colonial Williamsburg and is open to the public.

SAINT PAUL'S CHURCH, NORFOLK

The English imperialists who planted colonies in America tried repeatedly to encourage Virginians to congregate in towns, both for protection and to concentrate its tobacco exports in a few shipping centers. Some of the hoped-for towns—Jamestown, Yorktown, Tyndall's Point (Gloucester Point) and Port Royal—never grew large. However, Norfolk became an increasingly successful port after it was laid out in 1680, in response to Governor Culpeper's announcement that the King "is resolved as soon as storehouses and conveniences can be provided, to prohibit ships trading here to load or unload but at fixed places", including a site chosen in Lower Norfolk County on the Elizabeth River.

The King issued authorization for Norfolk's charter in 1736, calling for "a mayor, one person learned in the law styled and bearing the office of recorder of the said borough, eight aldermen, and sixteen other persons to be common-councilmen". Samuel Boush, a prosperous merchant, was named mayor and Sir John Randolph was appointed recorder. When he arrived to take office, "The gentlemen of the said town and neighborhood showed him all imaginable respect, by displaying the colors, and firing guns of the vessels lying there, and entertained him at their houses in the most elegant manner for several days, amply signalizing their great respect on this joyful occasion."

In 1739 a handsome borough church was built of brick on the west side of Church Street, described as "the only avenue by which the town could be entered by vehicles". It was so stoutly built that it survived the burning of Norfolk in the Revolution, although one wall was penetrated by a British cannon ball, fired during the bombardment of the town by Governor Lord Dunmore. Restored with funds raised by lottery in 1785, the church continued to serve Norfolk ever after. In 1832 its present name came in use to distinguish it from other Episcopal churches which were developing. It remains an active house of worship.

68

SAINT GEORGE TUCKER HOUSE

When the General Assembly amended the charter of William and Mary in 1779 at the instigation of Governor Jefferson, the ancient college added instruction in law, medicine and modern languages. The first professor of law was George Wythe, who was Williamsburg's most distinguished lawyer. However, Wythe also became judge of Virginia's Chancery Court and found it necessary to move with the capital to Richmond. He was succeeded as professor of law in 1790 by St. George Tucker, another eminent barrister.

Tucker had been born in Bermuda but moved to the colony as a young man. He attended William and Mary and was active as a patriot in the Revolution. His abilities won recognition as a lawyer, and in 1788 he was named judge of the General Court, which later became the Virginia Supreme Court of Appeals. He was dubbed "the American Blackstone" in 1803 after he published his annotated edition of Blackstone's *Commentaries on the Law*, which subsequent generations of law students made their bible.

The Saint George Tucker House, a detail of which is shown here, faces Williamsburg's Duke of Gloucester Street across the Courthouse Green. The long white frame house has a two-story-and-dormer central section, with lower wings. Five stairways occur in the "gunbarrel" house, which was probably first located on Palace Green and moved to its present site by Tucker.

Generations of the famous Tucker family of Virginia emanated from the spacious house, intermarrying with Randolphs, Lees, Blands and other families and bringing remarkable talent to the fields of law, medicine, theology and statecraft. The house was the scene of the first Christmas tree in Virginia and has welcomed distinguished guests. The picket fence and swinging gate shown here lead to the western wing with its great triangular chimney, only a stone's throw away from Palace Green.

GUNSTON HALL

One of Virginia's original thinkers of Revolutionary fame is George Mason, who in 1776 wrote the Virginia Declaration of Rights and thus inspired the Bill of Rights later appended to the Constitution. A serious man of deep learning and conviction, he was an early advocate of gradual emancipation of slaves and an agrarian liberal who feared the centralization of national power and the ascendancy of industry. Though a delegate to the Constitutional Convention, in Philadelphia in 1787, he refused to sign the document or support its ratification in Virginia because he felt that the agricultural states could not afford to give Congress the crucial power to control national commerce by simple majority vote and thus protect industry with tariffs.

Mason lived at Gunston Hall, a plantation in Fairfax County not far from Mount Vernon. The land was first patented in 1651 by Richard Turney, who was later hanged for taking part in Bacon's Rebellion in 1676. In 1696 Mason's grandfather acquired the land; the house was built by the great statesman himself, 1755–1758.

It contains beautifully designed mantels and molded plaster designs on its walls and ceilings, embodying Palladian and Chippendale designs. From its portico, its residents looked through a mammoth boxwood *allée*, surrounded by gardens, to the Potomac River beyond.

Acquired in recent years by the National Society of the Colonial Dames of America, the house is authentically furnished with rare and beautiful antiques of the period of Mason's lifetime. It is open to visitors daily.

72

CARTER'S GROVE

The oldest of Virginia's great mansions were those built along the James River, which remained the maritime thoroughfare of the Old Dominion until the wide spread of railroads after the Civil War. Among the James River houses, none has more perfect fusion of design, detail and site than Carter's Grove, the early seat of the Burwell family, a few miles east of Williamsburg. For more than two centuries it has entertained Royal Governors and Presidents. Here George Washington, Thomas Jefferson, Franklin D. Roosevelt and eminent men of other generations have been entertained in the lordly style of Virginia's one-time tobacco millionaires.

The house stands on land once owned by Robert "King" Carter, one of Virginia's wealthiest men, who owned more than 300,000 acres and 1000 slaves. It was he who specified in his will that the estate "in all times to come be called & to go by the name of Carter's Grove". His grandson Carter Burwell, a member of the House of Burgesses, began the house about 1750. So well and truly did he build—bringing a master woodworker from England, for example—that the house took six years to complete. In 1778 a young visitor from France, Madame Helene-Louise de Chastenay Maussion, wrote: ". . . we stopped at a famous place called Carter Grove, near James River, one of the most elegant habitations in Virginia. It is really a *beautiful* place." In more recent times author Samuel Chamberlain has called it "the most beautiful house in America".

Restored in the 1930's by the late Mr. and Mrs. Archibald McCrea, the house was recently acquired by the Rockefeller brothers and is maintained and exhibited by Colonial Williamsburg to illustrate the country life of Virginians. The handsome furnishings collected by Mr. and Mrs. McCrea are resplendent in such a setting.

74

THE NELSON HOUSE

It is fortunate for America that George Washington knew the geography of the Virginia Peninsula. For thus, when General the Lord Cornwallis marched his troops southward into Virginia in 1781 to join Britain's powerful naval force at Yorktown, the American commander realized the possibility of a Franco-American encirclement of Cornwallis' forces that would put an end to the Revolution.

Arriving in the village of Yorktown, Cornwallis commandeered as his headquarters the mansion of General Thomas Nelson, Jr., a merchant of the town who served for six months in 1781 as Governor of the harassed Commonwealth of Virginia. With unselfish patriotism, Nelson welcomed Washington's assault on Cornwallis' quarters as part of the siege that brought Cornwallis' capitulation on October 19, 1781. Nelson's house was badly damaged but later was restored to its early grandeur.

Built by the Nelson family in the 1730's, York Hall—as it was first called— is said to have had its cornerstone laid by young Thomas. Built in a form similar to that of Berkeley on the James, its thick walls are dressed in brick laid in Flemish bond design. Door moldings are of handsome rubbed brick, and the A roof and dormer windows are typical of Georgian houses of eighteenth-century England and her colonies.

Although he was the well-to-do grandson of the first Thomas Nelson, known as "Scotch Tom", who established the family trading interests in Yorktown, General Nelson suffered such financial losses in the Revolution that he died in straitened circumstances.

After having passed through several families, the Nelson House is today part of the Colonial National Historical Park, created by the National Park Service to link Jamestown, Williamsburg and Yorktown by the twenty-five-mile Colonial Parkway.

MOUNT VERNON

Of all Virginia's historic houses, Mount Vernon is of greatest interest. Each year, more than a million visitors see it, poised majestically on the banks of the Potomac in Fairfax County, a few miles from the District of Columbia. Owned and exhibited by the Mount Vernon Ladies' Association, it contains many of the furnishings, books and personal possessions which surrounded George and Martha Washington during their forty happy years of marriage, centering in this house and its thousands of surrounding acres.

Washington's great-grandfather, John, patented Mount Vernon's site in 1674, when northern Virginia was a thinly settled frontier. The property was particularly valuable because of the deep dockage afforded by the Potomac River to the ships which hauled Virginia's tobacco to England and Scotland. The estate was further developed by Augustine Washington, George's father, and Lawrence Washington, his brother, who named it for an admired English naval hero, Admiral Vernon. After Lawrence's death, George Washington acquired the handsome house and its acreage from his widow. There in 1759 he settled his bride, the former Martha Dandridge of New Kent County, who had been married to and widowed by Daniel Parke Custis. With them came Washington's two stepchildren, John Parke and Martha Parke Custis.

Though long absent as Commander-in-Chief of the Continental forces and later as President, Washington made his way as often as he could to his beloved acres. He personally directed the operation of this and his adjoining estates when he was in residence. On his death in 1799, he was buried in the family vault. Martha Washington died three years later, and in 1858 grateful Americans contributed funds with which to purchase the estate for exhibit to the public. House, outbuildings and grounds are maintained as Washington knew them— a handsome example of a wealthy Virginia planter's home.

78

THE MOORE HOUSE

Yorktown was the chief York River port in the seventeenth century, as Jamestown was on the James. Around it were clustered a few warehouses, stores, merchants' house and plantations like Edward Digges', which grew the highly prized sweet-scented tobacco. One of the early merchants was Augustine Moore, who built a handsome gambrel-roof house a mile east of the town, on the banks of the river.

Although it is similar in size and shape to several Williamsburg houses, the Augustine Moore House is a landmark in America history. It was here that the Articles of Capitulation were drafted by the Continental and French armies, commanded by Washington and Rochambeau, after the surrender of General the Lord Cornwallis, commanding the British forces. This event, on October 18, 1781, signaled the end of British power in America and led in two years to the signing of the Treaty of Paris, recognizing the independence of the American colonies.

In accordance with the agreement drawn up in the Moore House, Cornwallis' sword was presented to the Allies on October 19, signifying his surrender. Then the humbled red-coated army marched out of Yorktown at two o'clock in the afternoon, between the French and American armies, and laid down their arms. The victory was gloriously celebrated that night in the taverns of Yorktown and Williamsburg, only twelve miles from the surrender scene.

Today Yorktown is part of the Colonial National Historical Park, preserved for posterity by the National Park Service. The Moore House and other surviving structures are exhibited to the public, while the inner circle of defenses, dug by the British when they found themselves surrounded, have been reconstructed and marked. Also rebuilt are the siege battlements of the Americans and French. Visitors are shown the battle lines and the disposition of the offshore French and British battle fleets from the National Park Service Information Center in the heart of Cornwallis' doomed stronghold.

BRUSH-EVERARD HOUSE

One of the many original buildings of Williamsburg still standing is the dormered wooden house built by John Brush in 1717 on the Palace Green, close by the handsome new Governor's Palace. Here lived the first keeper of the colony's powder magazine, located on nearby Market Square. Brush apparently carried on his business as gunsmith and armorer in his house, as did many Williamsburg craftsmen.

But time passes and houses change hands. In 1742 the property was bought by William Dering, teacher of dancing at the College of William and Mary. A more influential owner was Thomas Everard, who was clerk of York County, nearby, from 1745 until his death in 1784. For a time he was also auditor of Virginia and clerk of the General Court, serving for a while as mayor. It was he, no doubt, who enlarged the house with a one-story rear addition and refurbished the interior. Perhaps he was also responsible for the handsome staircase, which is ornamented with carving similar to that at Carter's Grove and at Tuckahoe, in Goochland County.

The first-floor front room shown here has paneled wainscoting, a Turkey carpet and typical mid-eighteenth century furnishings of a well-to-do Williamsburg household. In an adjoining room a library has been assembled on the basis of Thomas Jefferson's list, compiled in 1771, for the guidance of a well-to-do planter. The 300 volumes range from the classics to drama, history, law, philosophy, religion and science. The house is one of the many exhibition buildings which are kept open to the public by Colonial Williamsburg.

KENMORE

One of the centers of colonial Virginia life was Fredericksburg, on the Rappahannock River. Strategically located close to the Shenandoah Mountains of northern Virginia, it was a port of entry for many English, Scotch-Irish and German settlers in Virginia's second century. After an overnight stay in one of Fredericksburg's inns, the emigrants usually boarded a stagecoach for the upland drive to Winchester or some Valley of Virginia settlement where land was for sale.

George Washington lived as a boy at Ferry Farm, across the Rappahannock from the town. James Monroe began his career as a country lawyer there. Dr. Hugh Mercer, a Scottish émigré who kept an office and apothecary shop, became a general in the Continental Army. A young Scotsman named John Paul came to live with his brother, a tailor in the town, and later became famous as John Paul Jones in the Revolutionary navy.

Among the homes built on the heights overlooking the river was Kenmore, the seat of an 863-acre flax-and-tobacco plantation. To it came Betty Washington in 1752 as the wife of Colonel Fielding Lewis, who during the Revolution was in charge of the Fredericksburg Arms Manufactory that supplied Virginia's soldiery.

Handsomely paneled and furnished, Kenmore is maintained as an exhibit today by the Kenmore Association. It contains many objects owned by the Lewises, as well as countless associations with the Washington and Ball families. For history-lovers, the home of Mary Ball Washington, mother of the first President, stands nearby. Other historic buildings to be seen include Hugh Mercer's Apothecary Shop, James Monroe's law library, the Rising Sun Tavern and the Masonic Lodge which Washington joined in 1752. Fredericksburg is indeed a city with a romantic past.

84

WOODLAWN PLANTATION

Close to Alexandria stands Woodlawn, built in 1805. On an estate given by George and Martha Washington to her granddaughter, Eleanor Parke Custis, she and her husband, Lawrence Lewis, built a Palladian-style house designed for them by William Thornton, first architect of the United States Capitol. A century later it became the home of Senator Oscar Underwood. It is now maintained for the public by the National Trust for Historic Preservation.

The house stands on a ridge facing the distant Potomac. It has the ampleness and sense of solidity of the earlier Georgian plantations, but it also has characteristics of the Italian villas designed by the Renaissance Italian architect, Andreas Palladio, which were copied in England and popularized in America at the end of the eighteenth century, notably by Thomas Jefferson at Monticello.

Woodlawn is furnished with articles given to Colonel Lewis, who was George Washington's nephew, and his wife by the Washingtons, together with other beautiful items of the period. They are characterized by the refinement and delicacy of French décor of the period, which remembered with fondness the revolutionary efforts of such French allies as Lafayette, Rochambeau and de Grasse.

Woodlawn's garden has been restored through proceeds received by the Garden Club of Virginia from its annual Garden Week.

SHERWOOD FOREST PLANTATION

When John Tyler retired from the Presidency of the United States in 1845, he described himself as an outlaw, like Robin Hood. He had differed with his fellow Whigs, by whom he had been elected Vice-President on the ticket with William Henry Harrison, and he was anathema to the other parties as well. He renamed his Charles City County home Sherwood Forest and went there with his recent bride, the former Julia Gardiner, of New York, to nurse his political wounds.

Although he bought the house in 1842, while still President, Tyler was a lifelong resident of James City County, between Williamsburg and Richmond. Born at nearby Greenway, he had served in county and state political office before entering national politics. Nearby lived the Harrison family, whose restless son William Henry had migrated into the Northwestern Territory, won fame along the Canadian border in the War of 1812 and been elected President in 1842 with the battle-cry, "Tippecanoe and Tyler Too".

A frame house of simple planter style, Sherwood Forest is not as pretentious as some of the great houses of earlier Virginia. However, it is impressive in its wide façade and descendants of President Tyler still live beneath its roof. The house is open to the public.

JOHN MARSHALL HOUSE

A pleasant surprise in the heart of downtown Richmond is the home of Chief Justice John Marshall, at the intersection of Ninth and Marshall streets. There the tall attorney and his wife, Mary Ambler "Polly" Marshall, built their Federal-style townhouse in 1790, and there he found his greatest happiness for the remaining forty-five years of his career. Later and more delicate in detail than most houses of Virginia's "Great Generation", the Marshall House is handsomely furnished with heirlooms of the Ambler and Marshall families, collected by the Association for the Preservation of Virginia Antiquities from numerous heirs. The house is open Tuesday through Sunday.

Richmond was a simple James River trading town in 1780, when the Virginia Assembly moved the seat of government from Williamsburg. Most of its houses then stood on Church Hill, whose topmost height was dominated by the white spire of St. John's Episcopal Church. However, when the site for the new Capitol was chosen atop the adjoining Shockoe Hill, this area became the most desirable location for new homes. There the Marshalls built.

A number of able men were attracted to Richmond in this growing era, but none surpassed Marshall in the breadth and penetration of his mind. Though not as scholarly as his distant cousin Jefferson, nor as witty as another mutual kinsman, John Randolph of Roanoke, Marshall was capable of intense concentration and penetration. Perhaps best of all, he was a man of independent mind who held to his convictions at any cost.

Though Polly Marshall's lifelong nervous ailment precluded much entertainment, the Chief Justice was exceedingly popular among the Richmond men who gathered on Saturdays to play quoits. His simplicity of manner and dress was often noted, sometimes unfavorably by people surprised to see the Chief Justice carrying a live fowl home from market.

FORTRESS MONROE

Fortress Monroe was built between 1819 and 1834 at the tip of the Virginia Peninsula, to protect the portals of Chesapeake Bay. Its huge coastal guns have roared in anger only once—during the Civil War—but they are a grim reminder of the days when Americans expected imminent attack on coastal shipping. Built before the atomic era, the fort has the frowning gun-ports and even the moat which protected medieval castles. But it continues to serve a purpose. Headquartered within it is the United States Army's Continental Army Command, which is responsible for the defense of the American continent.

Fortress Monroe was projected in the administration of President James Monroe. John C. Calhoun, then Secretary of War, pressed its completion for fear of another attack similar to that which the British made on Craney Island and Hampton in the War of 1812. However, the tremendous labor and expense of the project greatly delayed its completion. Designed by General Simon Bernard of the French army, it was thought so strong that it was called "the Gibraltar of the Chesapeake". It remained a center of Federal strength during the Civil War and later was the scene of the imprisonment of former Confederate President Jefferson Davis. Falsely accused at first of plotting Lincoln's assassination, Davis was finally cleared and released. A museum has been made of the Davis casemate.

Fortress Monroe stands on the site of Fort Algernon, which was built in 1609 by the Jamestown settlers as a coast-watching outpost for the settlement thirty miles up the James River. In the eighteenth century, it was succeeded by a larger outpost, Fort George, named for England's King George I. After the fort was destroyed by a typhoon in 1749—commanded by Major Samuel Barron, whose sons and grandsons became famous sailing-ship captains—Old Point Comfort remained unfortified until Fortress Monroe was built. Visitors to the fortress today may see quarters which once housed Edgar Allan Poe, Robert E. Lee and famous commanders of World War I and II.

WHITE HOUSE OF THE CONFEDERACY

When the Virginia Assembly built Virginia's new Capitol in Richmond in 1787–1788 in the style of the Maison Carrée, an ancient Roman temple at Nismes, France, it introduced the revival of classical architecture that swept nineteenth-century America. This was the style chosen by Dr. John Brockenbrough for the handsome townhouse he built in 1818 at the "Court End" of Richmond, looking out over Shockoe Valley to the face of Church Hill.

A member of the powerful "Essex Junto" composed of Chief Justice Spencer Roane of the Virginia Court of Appeals, editor Thomas Ritchie of the Richmond *Enquirer* and others, Brockenbrough was host to many of the Jeffersonian party leaders of Virginia—though perhaps not many of John Marshall's opposing Federalist partisans. After the Brockenbroughs' lifetime, the city of Richmond bought the house in 1861, and it became the official residence of President Jefferson Davis of the Confederate States until 1865.

Though Richmond's "Court End" is no longer a fashionable residential area—having become the demesne of the Medical College of Virginia and many offices—it retains enough of its ante-bellum houses to preserve the Civil War flavor. The Brockenbrough house is now open to the public as the Confederate Museum. It houses thousands of battle flags, guns and other mementos of the Civil War, together with furnishings appropriate to the period of the Davises' residence.

The house is open on weekdays from 9 to 5 and on Sunday from 2 to 5. Nearby are other early Richmond homes, including the Poe Museum, the Valentine Museum, the John Marshall House and General Lee's wartime residence. Also well worth a visit are St. John's Church and the restored Church Hill homes and their mews.